designs for
machine
embroidery

designs for machine embroidery

IRA LILLOW

B. T. BATSFORD LIMITED, London & Sydney

ISBN 0 7134 3023 0

Filmset by Servis Filmsetting Limited, Manchester
Printed and bound in Great Britain by
The Pitman Press, Bath
for the publishers
B T BATSFORD LIMITED
4 Fitzhardinge Street, London W1H 0AH
and
23 Cross Street Brookvale NSW 2100 Australia

contents

acknowledgment

I wish to thank Mr Peter Wood for his kind help with the photography for this book.

introduction

This book is intended as a source of inspiration for designs in machine embroidery. It is almost impossible to teach design as such because so much depends on the individual worker, on her likes and dislikes, her previous experience of design and her appreciation of shape and colour. Therefore various ways of developing design and ideas are shown; these can be further developed and perhaps repeated in order to produce larger and more intricate designs. The designs in this book should not necessarily be copied; instead careful study should be made to see how they were evolved. These designs can be produced in the same way, but with differing results to the original.

Inspiration for embroidery can come from many sources. One such source is natural form found in plants and animals: instead of looking at these as a whole, examine detailed features, for example cross sections showing the inside of fruit and vegetables, close-up views of leaves, petals and cell structure. Shadows and water often form interesting shapes. Experiments can be made by shining light through transparent materials to cast unusual shadows. Light playing on running water or through a glass of crushed ice can also inspire designs. The natural formation of rocks, stones and fossils can create pleasing shapes as well as giving an idea of texture. There are endless sources of ideas.

Machine embroidery is a fascinating pastime and the most necessary requirement is patience, particularly at first, because the machine may run away with itself and produce stitching where it was never intended to be. With plenty of practice this will not happen; however, the runaway stitches can give an unintentional but interesting effect. This is the reason why a machine embroidery can be so exciting and spontaneous, and sometimes even more effective than the original design. It is because of this that a beginner can produce such stimulating work. With more and more practice the work can be so attractive and full of colour that even a hand embroiderer must admire its beauty.

The techniques of machine embroidery are discussed only very briefly here; several books dealing with this subject are listed in the bibliography. It is important that the embroiderer should be familiar with her machine and know how to adapt it for this type of embroidery before she launches out on any major piece of work. As with any art form so much depends on the quality of the material, the colours chosen, and particularly on the well-prepared design.

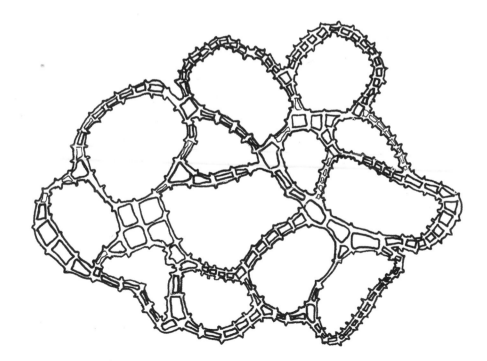

adapting a machine

1 An electric machine must be used so that both hands are free to manoeuvre the fabric.

2 The feed teeth, which normally help to push the fabric along, must be lowered so that the machining can be moved freely in any direction. The sewing machine booklet will show how to do this: on most modern machines there is simply a knob to turn or a button to press. With an old machine there may be a metal plate that can be screwed down over the teeth so that they cannot operate. If this proves difficult ask for help at your nearest sewing machine supplier.

3 Remove the foot altogether so that the needle stands alone.

4 For beginners it is advisable to work on a small area at first until proper control of the machine is achieved. The fabric should be held taut in an embroidery hoop. Metal or wooden hoops can be used, but wooden ones should be bound for greater efficiency. More advanced machine embroiderers working over larger areas, will find that a small darning foot attachment can be used instead of an embroidery hoop; in this case the entire fabric has to be pulled and pushed under the needle. This is quite difficult and should only be attempted by the more experienced.

how to begin

1 Thread up the machine in the normal way using the same thickness of thread on the top and the bottom.

Machine embroidery thread of varying thickness depending on the type of fabric can be used; a finer thread for delicate fabrics and a thicker one for heavier fabrics. A 40 *Sylko* can be used on most types of fabrics. It is not necessary to adjust the tension for ordinary stitching, and since the feed teeth do not operate, neither will the stitch gauge, and it is unnecessary to adjust that either.

2 Lower the feed teeth and remove the foot.

3 Make sure that the fabric is taut in the embroidery hoop, with the right side inside (the opposite way from that used for hand embroidery).

4 Put the embroidery hoop under the needle with the flat side (wrong side) downwards and lower the presser foot lever. This can easily be forgotten because there is no foot on the machine. Put the needle down into the fabric to bring the under thread to the surface. Hold the threads taut for the first few stitches to prevent the machine jamming, then cut them off.

5 Because there are no feed teeth to push the fabric along, this has to be done by moving the hoop backwards and forwards under the needle. As the stitch operator is not working, when the hoop is moved quickly a large stitch is obtained, and when it is moved slowly, a small one.

6 Continue machining, moving the hoop wherever in any direction, using the needle as a pen to draw on to the fabric.

various stitching techniques

These are line exercises for the beginner. Keep the embroidery taut in the hoop, use the machine as a pen, and draw these lines on to the fabric.

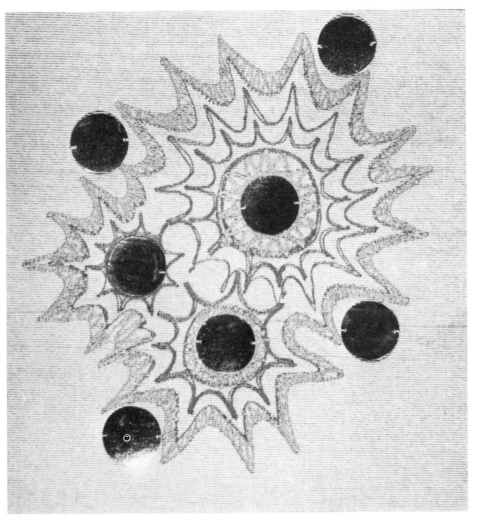

This piece of free embroidery is a good practice sample, involving loop stitch and swinging curves. It is a simple motif that could be filled in with more detail and used on a garment, or possibly on the lid of a box or a cushion.

The two motifs on the opposite and the following page are also good practice samples. In the first simple shape (*opposite*) the machine embroidery threads only are used, and the spaces are filled in with loop stitch, seeding and a little free zigzag stitch. This stitch is carried out in the same way as for normal free embroidery, but it involves setting the gauge at a zigzag stitch and it requires quite considerable machine control.

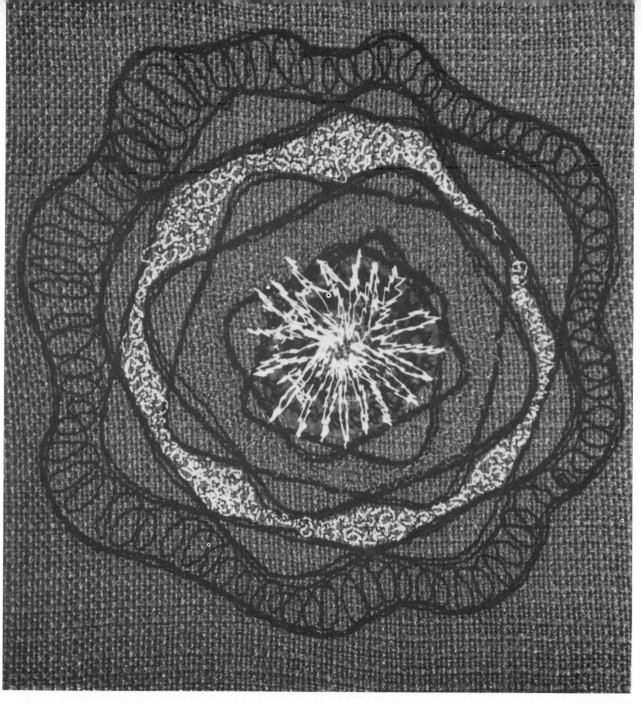

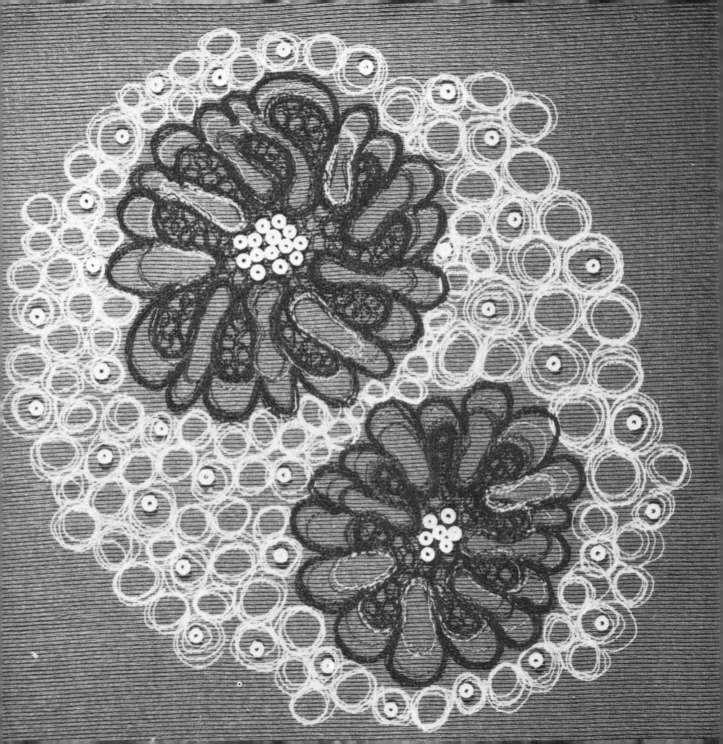

The second motif (*left*) shows small circular shapes which can be built up effectively to cover small areas. Small beads are added to echo the circular shapes.

Working on velvet, corduroy or any fabrics with a pile can prove disasterous, as much of the work tends to be lost in the pile. If such a fabric must be used, always choose a fine quality and not one with a deep pile.

Hand embroidery, couched threads and felt appliqué are included in this piece of embroidery. The machine embroidery would be lost in the pile of the velvet if hand embroidery were not used as well.

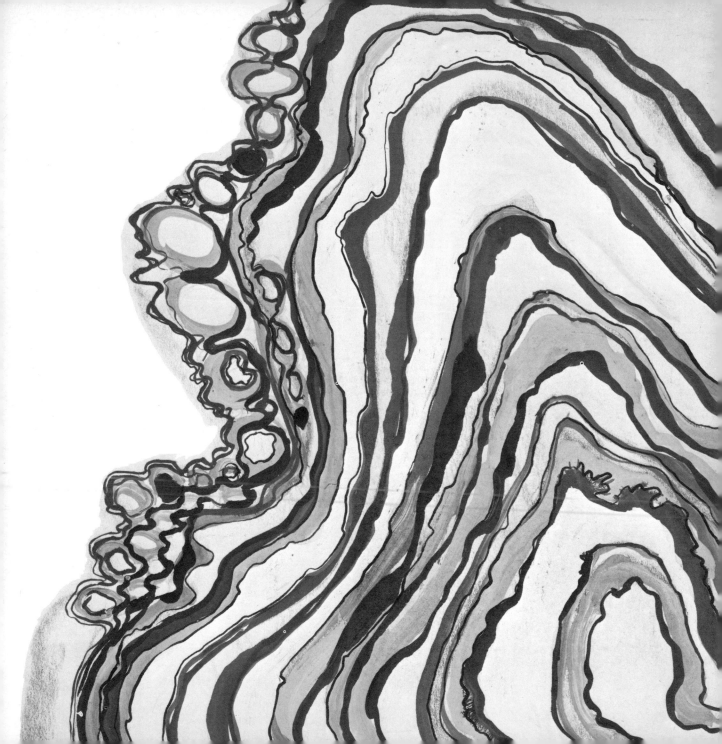

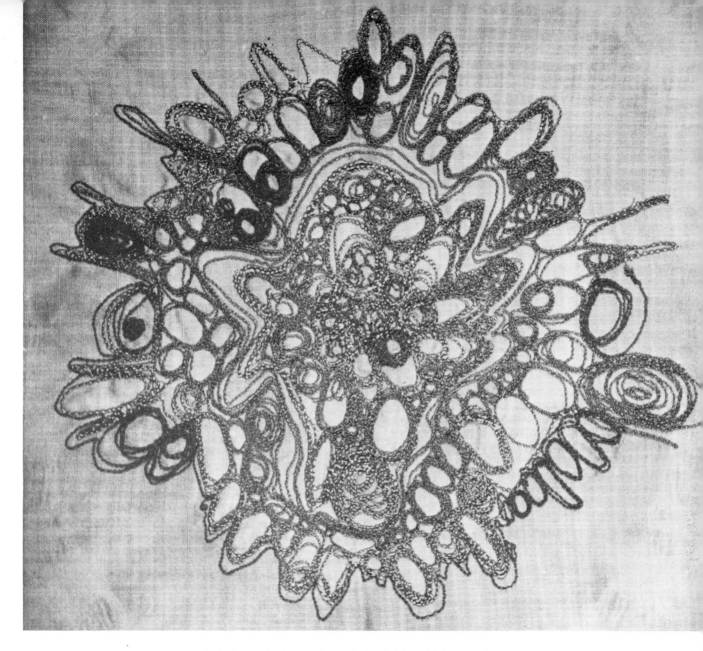

This is worked on a tie-and-dye fabric which can give an interesting background for a large piece of work. In this work a different coloured thread was used on the bottom shuttle from the one on the top reel, and the tension loosened slightly.

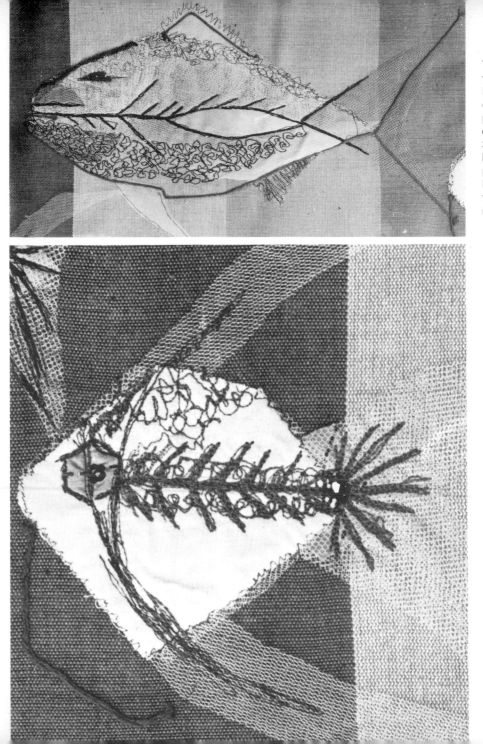

This fish panel shows some very simple machine embroidery that any beginner can attempt. The fish on this page are made from layers of fabric and nylon net. Simple seeding, which can be seen here, is an excellent practice stitch because one has to work slowly to fill up the spaces where it is required.

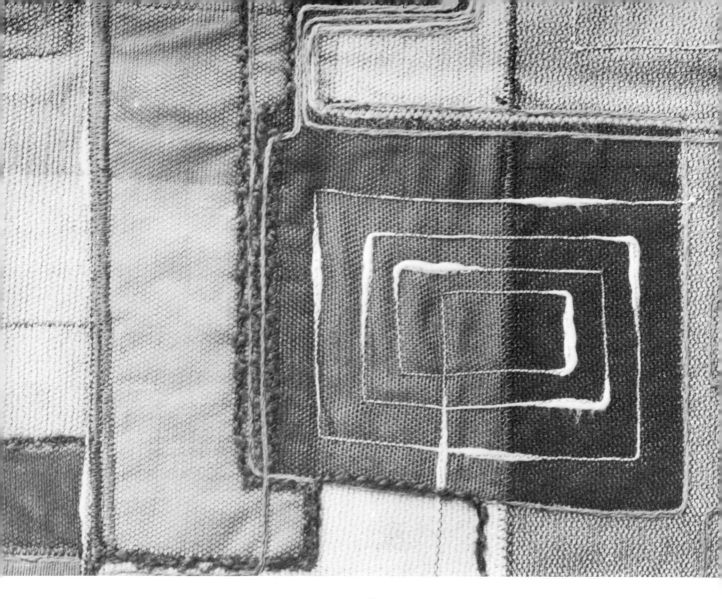

This panel is made up from a wide variety of fabrics of differing textures, and stitched down with an over-locking stitch which alters in width. Many of the shapes are outlined with textured threads couched down with the machine. There is no free embroidery on this panel; it is worked entirely with the foot on the machine and the feed teeth in operation.

This is a simple exercise using tape and bindings and a varying width of over-locking stitch. It provides good practice for gaining control of the machine.

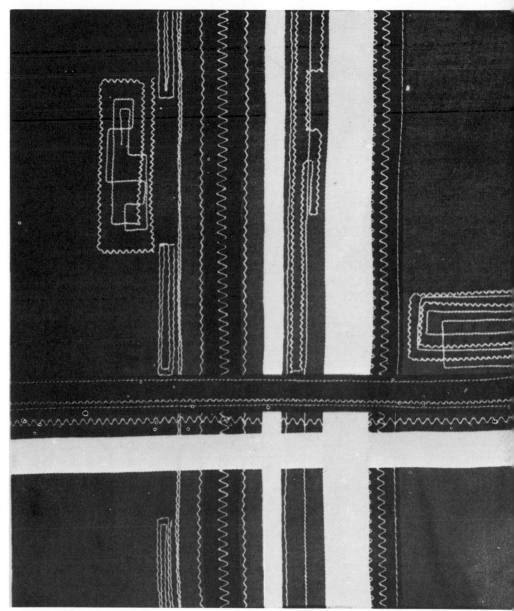

(*opposite*) Detail of the previous panel using applied textured fabrics and couched threads.

This design could be worked in applied fabrics, braids, tapes and bindings, couched threads and straight and zigzag machining.

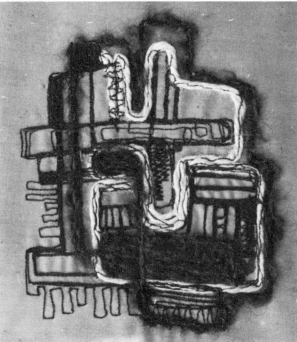

Textured threads couched down with the machine, and free embroidery for the filling, were used to produce this geometric design.

This is another design that could be developed in the
same way, using appliquéed shapes and heavy textured
threads couched down with machining. The fine lines
on the design could be made with free machine
embroidery.

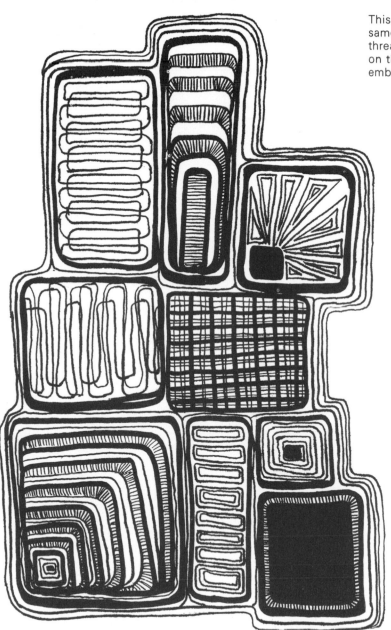

transferring the designs on to the fabric

1 Working freely.
A design can be transferred straight on to the background fabric simply by looking at the finished sketch while machining. In this way a spontaneous effect can be achieved; not exactly like the original, but very attractive.

2 Applique and machine embroidery.
If the design, or parts of it, are to be appliquéed on to the background fabric, draw the design again on tracing paper, cut out the shapes which are to be appliqueed and use these as patterns for cutting out the selected pieces of material. Lightly paste or tack (baste) them into place. Pasting the pieces on to the background fabric is a satisfactory way of holding them in place temporarily until they are machined. It also saves the time wasted unpicking tacking stitches which inevitably get caught in with the embroidery stitches. When most of the design has been applied in this way, the machining can be worked freely as the position of the design will have been determined by the appliquéed shapes.

3 Tracing.
Trace the design on to tracing paper and tack the entire piece on to the background fabric around the edge of the paper. Machine the outline of the design and any of the main lines within it. When a good impression of the design has been machined, tear away the paper and continue machining freely.
One can also trace the design on to the background fabric through smear-proof carbon paper, the type used in dressmaking. If this is done the carbon mark must be completely covered with embroidery, otherwise it may spoil the outline produced by the machine stitches.

4 Using a pencil.
The design can also be sketched lightly on to the background fabric, following the outline as carefully as possible. Take care not to use indelible pencil. Do not try to sketch too much at once because the drawing tends to wear away as it is worked on. Draw only the outline first, machine this in, then fill in the details. The outline can always be sketched on to the wrong side and machined in, the fabric is then reversed and the machining continued in detail.

developing
the designs
Using natural form

Natural form can provide all the inspiration necessary
to create hundreds of designs. One can draw realistic
designs from nature which appeal to many people, or
one can use natural shapes and line from which to draw
abstract designs.

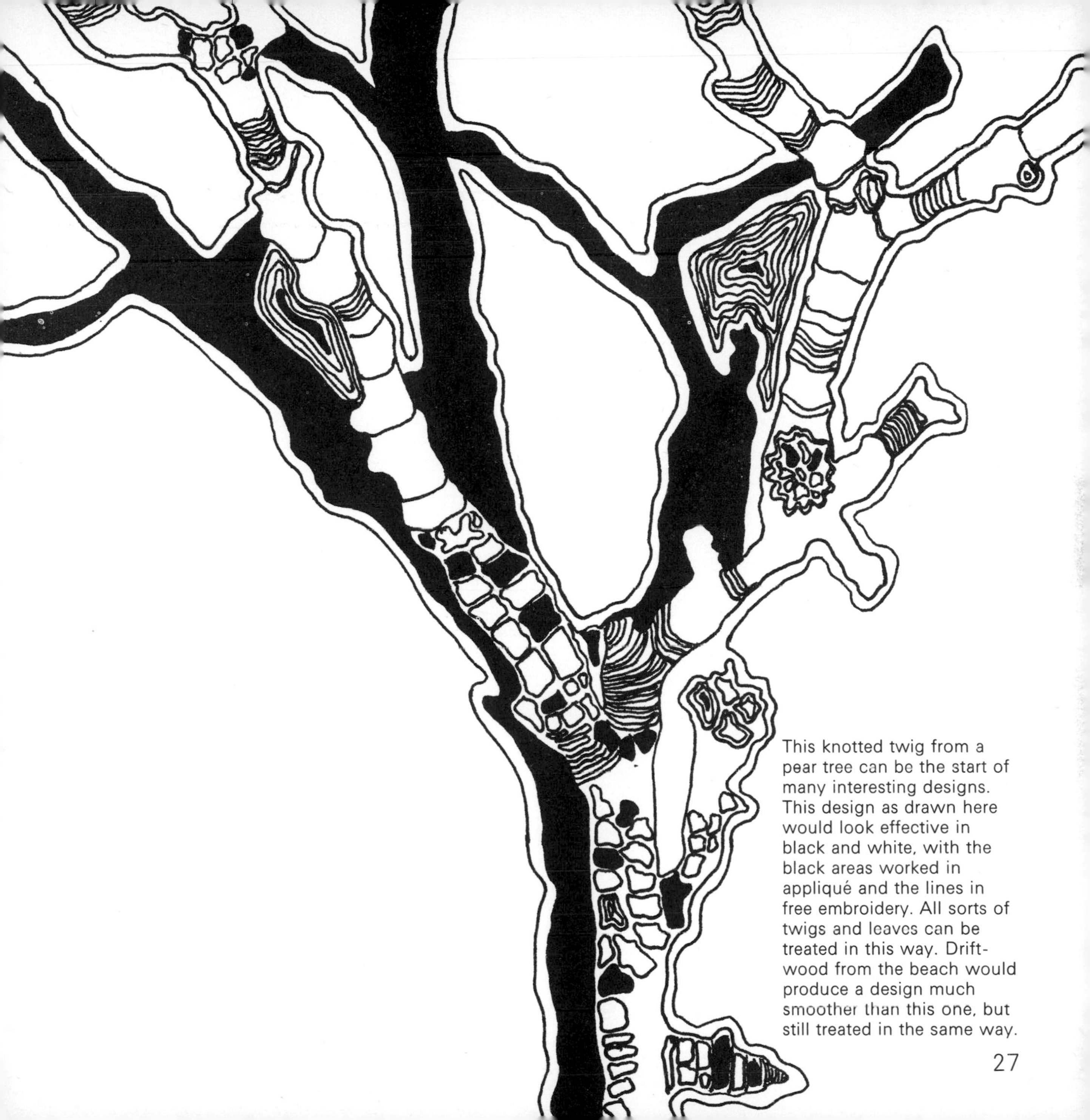

This knotted twig from a pear tree can be the start of many interesting designs. This design as drawn here would look effective in black and white, with the black areas worked in appliqué and the lines in free embroidery. All sorts of twigs and leaves can be treated in this way. Driftwood from the beach would produce a design much smoother than this one, but still treated in the same way.

27

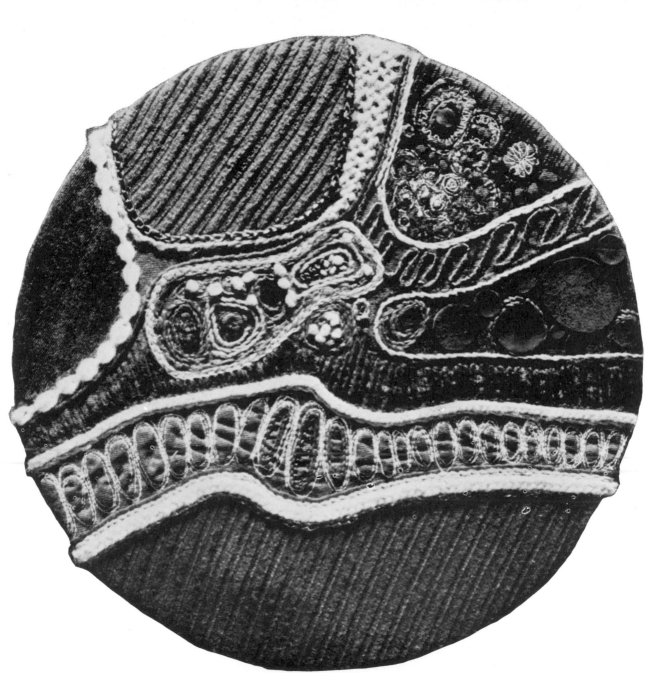

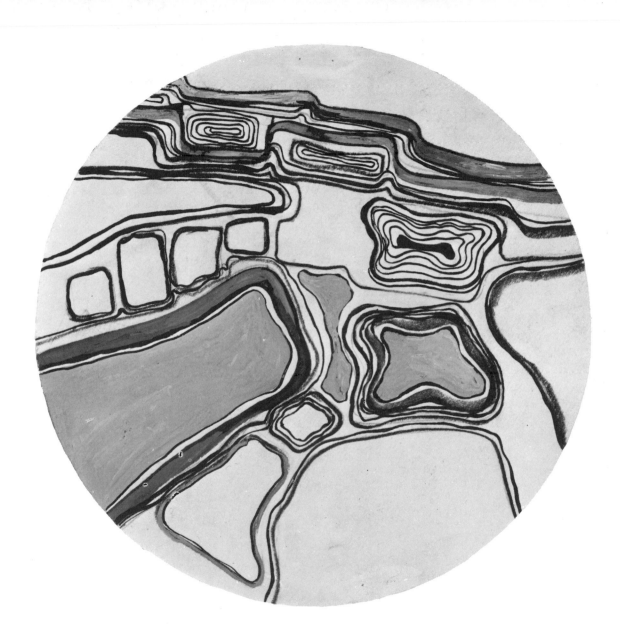

The following three designs are also developed from twig shapes and tree bark. The embroidery on the facing page is made up of machine and hand embroidery with couched threads and cords, together with velvet appliqué and suede circles glued on.

Bark . . . a simple exercise
for contour line embroidery.

These seed pods are a typical example of how natural form can be applied in an abstract way to develop the most exciting and intricate designs. They can be worked in their natural colours or can be further abstracted by using a range of colour not generally associated with the object.

PLATE 1.
Small circular shapes which can be built up effectively to cover small areas. Small beads are added to echo the circular shapes.

This seed pod can be effectively interpreted in smooth and textured fabrics and a great deal of machine embroidery.

A seed pod design. This
would be suitable for line
embroidery.

33

This seed pod design can be used to produce a simple abstract shape by drawing only the main outlines and adding a few more contour lines. The shapes can be filled in with embroidery or appliqué, or both. This may well produce a piece of work quite unlike the seed pod which was the original inspiration for the design.

34

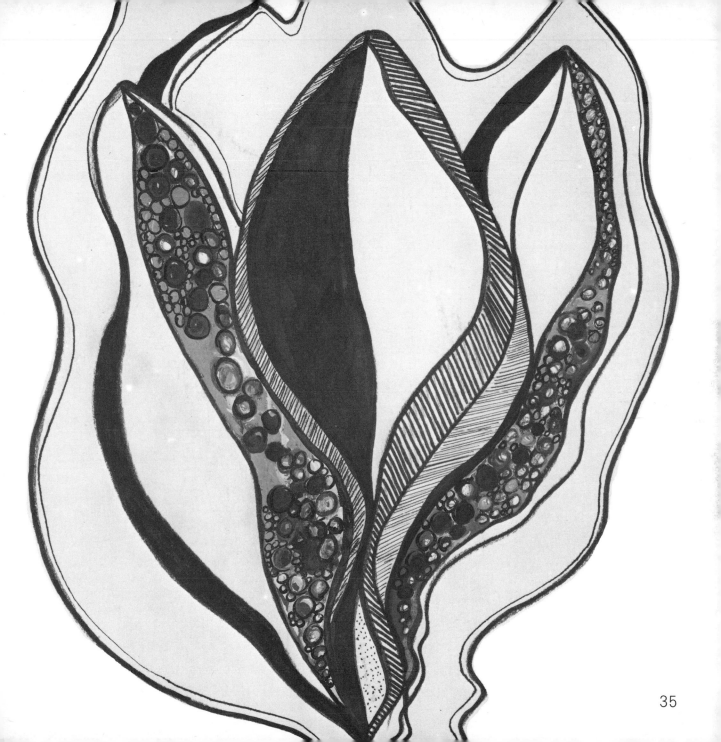

35

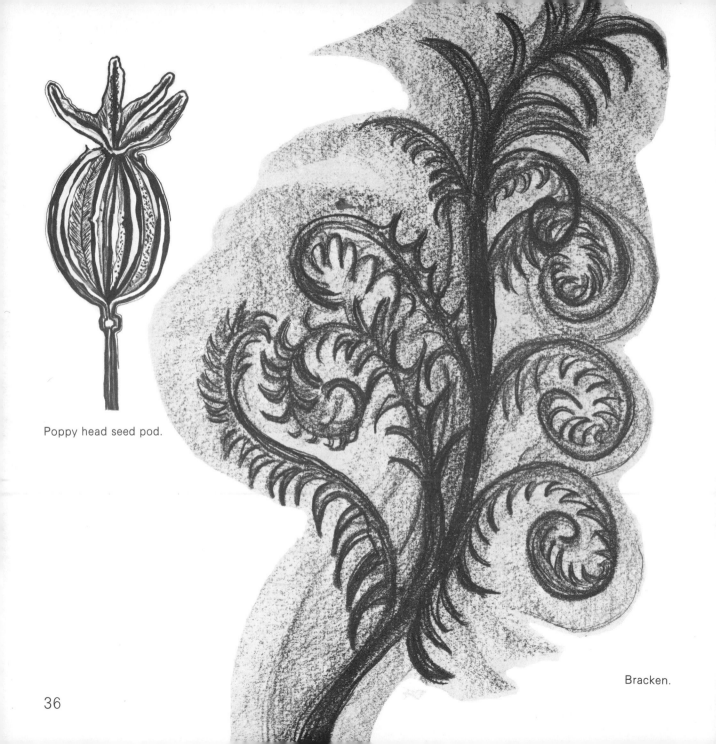

Poppy head seed pod.

Bracken.

36

The following three
designs are typical
of those one can
draw without
having the objects
available. This is a drawing-
from-memory exercise,
letting the imagination run
away with one. Think of an
object and draw what you
think it looks like. This
method can often produce
lively imaginative designs.

Half a melon.

Half an onion.

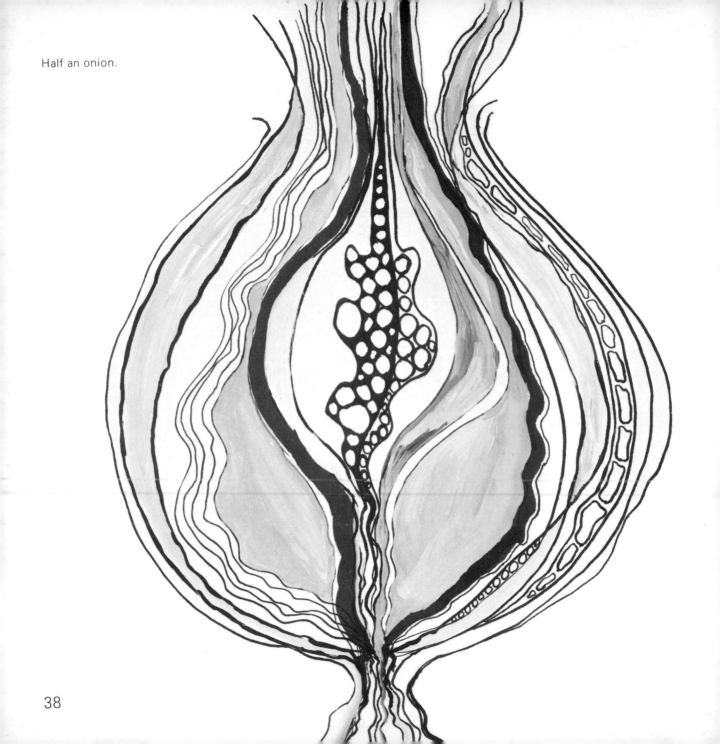

Half an apple.

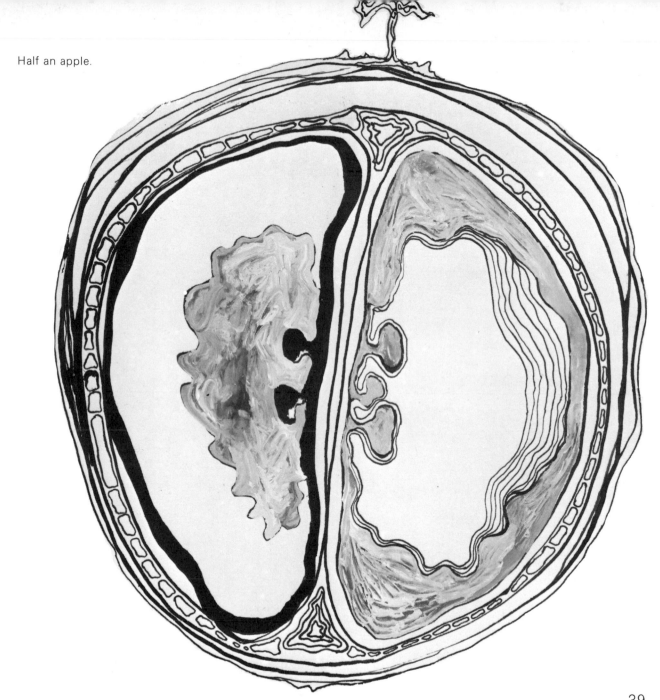

This design is of a shell found on the beach. It has been built up with simple lines of machining in various colours and bands of chain stitch.

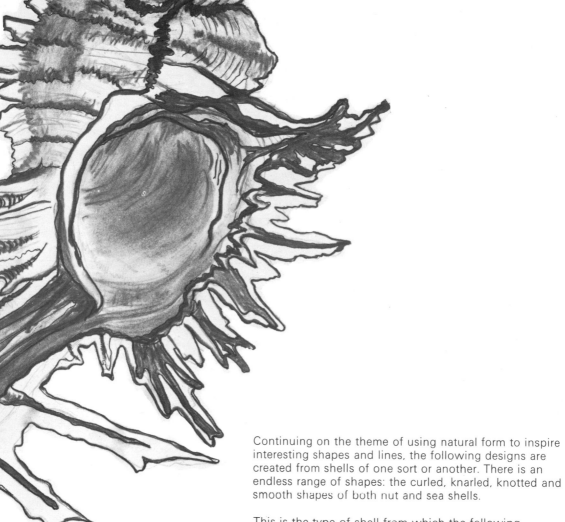

Continuing on the theme of using natural form to inspire interesting shapes and lines, the following designs are created from shells of one sort or another. There is an endless range of shapes: the curled, knarled, knotted and smooth shapes of both nut and sea shells.

This is the type of shell from which the following design was taken. It gives excellent scope for machine embroidery because it is so full of detail.

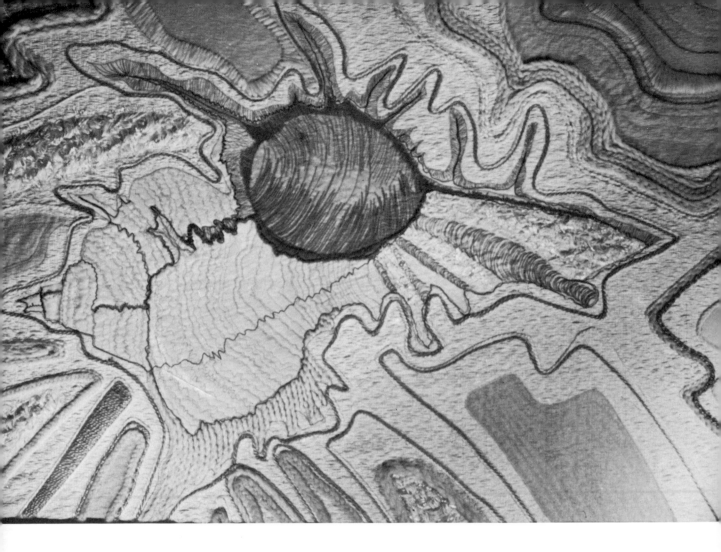

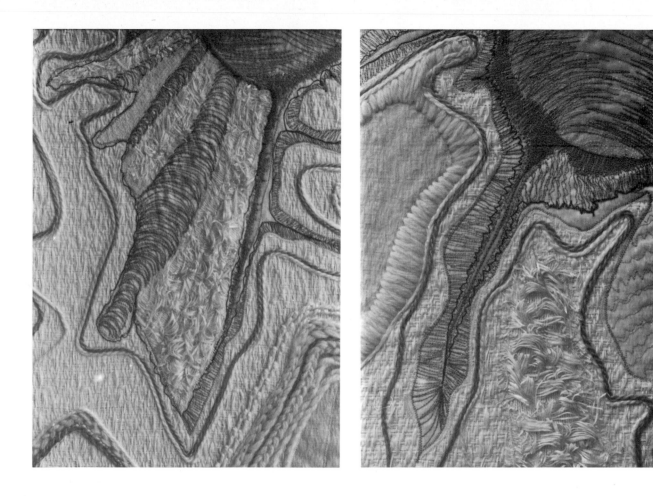

This panel is worked mainly in white, cream and beige with a little pink and dark brown where the shell changes colour towards the inside. The whole embroidery is worked on white strawcloth with several heavier strawcloths qppliquéed on in various places. Although machine embroidery dominates the panel, there is also a great deal of hand embroidery worked in heavy threads, thus creating a wide variety of texture over the whole piece of work.

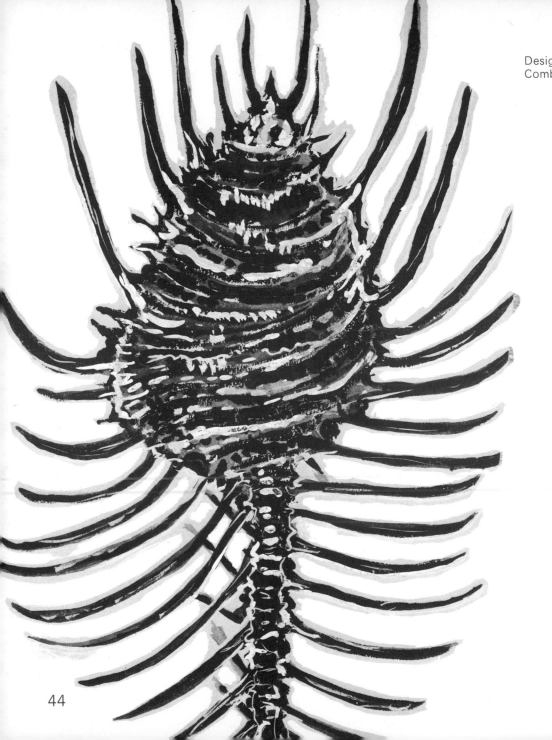

Design inspired by a Venus Comb Murex.

44

This design is from a sea-worn oyster type of shell, which, although much battered by the sea, still had traces of pearly surface to it. It provides quite a challenge to the machine embroiderer.

An abstract design inspired by snail shells.

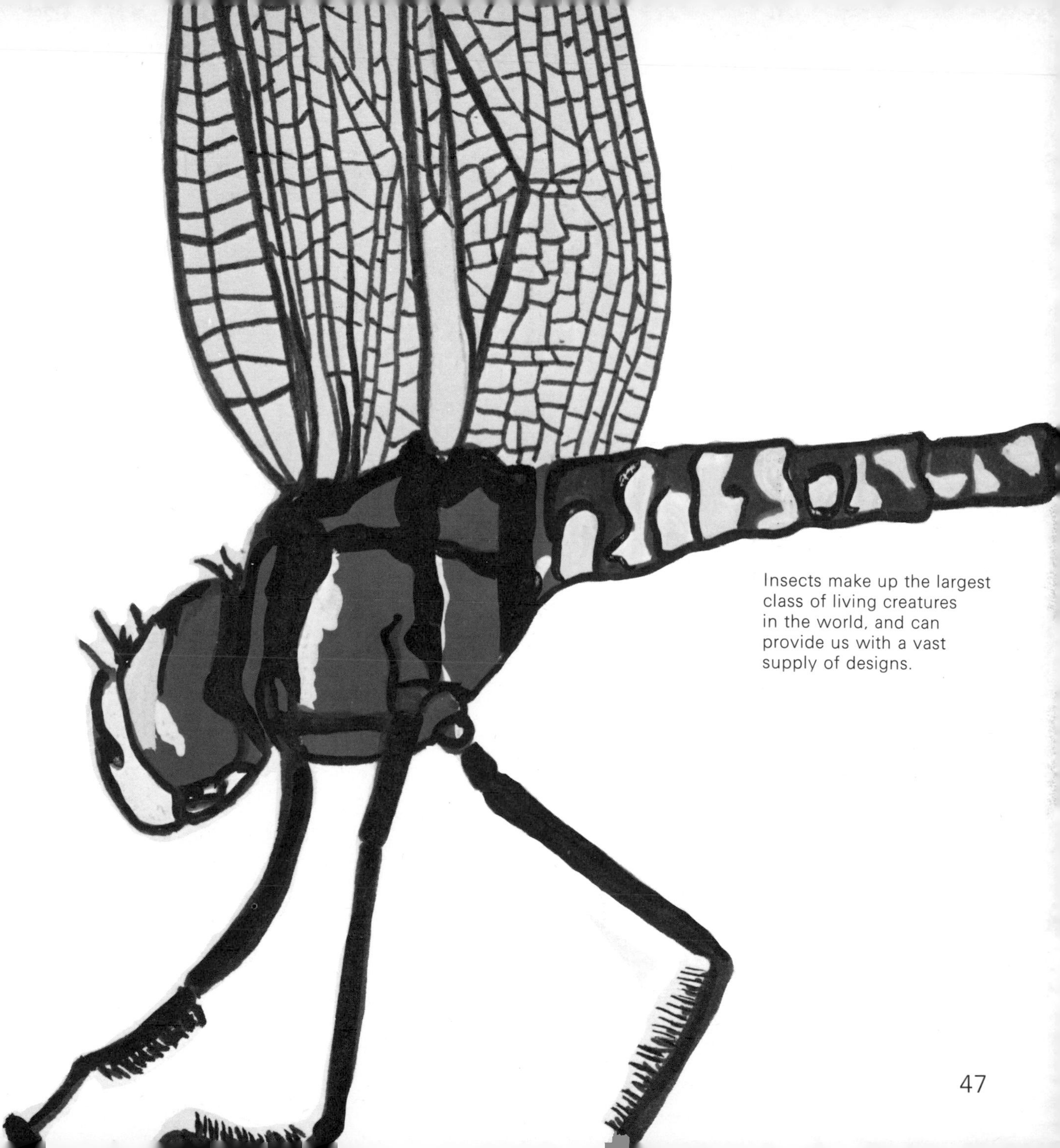

Insects make up the largest
class of living creatures
in the world, and can
provide us with a vast
supply of designs.

These two designs are
worked in machine threads
only but in a wide variety of
brilliant colours.

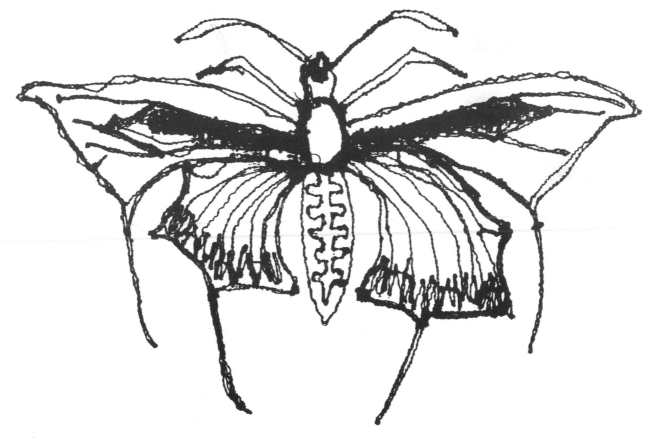

An abstract design of insect wings.

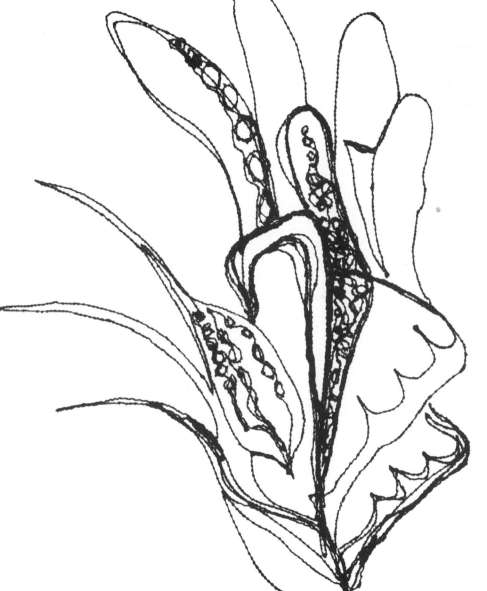

PLATE 2.
A simple exercise using tape and bindings and a varying width of overlocking stitch. It provides good practice for gaining control of the machine.

The following drawings show how more realistic and detailed designs can be worked in free machine embroidery, using several different colours. Applied fabrics could be included, as in the crab where the reverse of the background fabric has been used.

Gold threads are machined into this design. The thread is wound on to the bobbin and the machining is worked from the wrong side; that is, the piece of fabric is taken out of the hoop and replaced the reverse side up. This method is more effective than threading the top of the machine with the gold thread, because it tends to break as it passes through the needle.

A sea-worn shell, showing the various channels inside it.

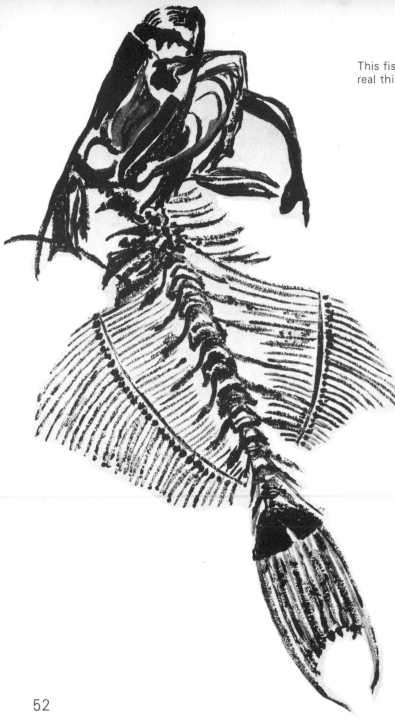

This fish skeleton was painted from a photograph of the real thing.

Looking at creatures in a natural camouflage, such as these tortoises, can provide a combination of lines where the background lines merge with the objects.

Flowerheads.

This piece of embroidery is
made from bunched-up
pieces of fabric, machine
and hand embroidery,
couched textured threads
and beads.

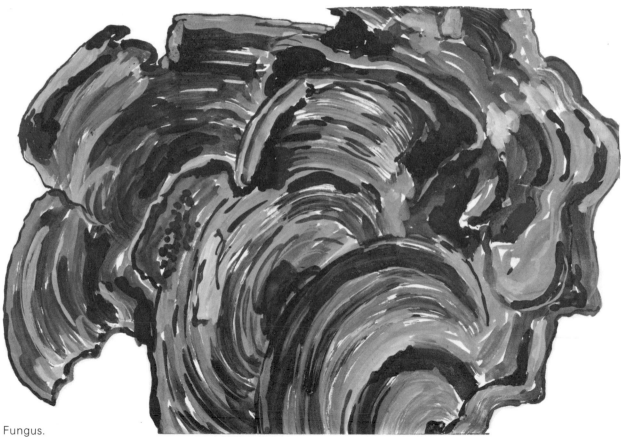

Fungus.

A wide variety of shapes and curves are evident when fruit and vegetables are cut in half.

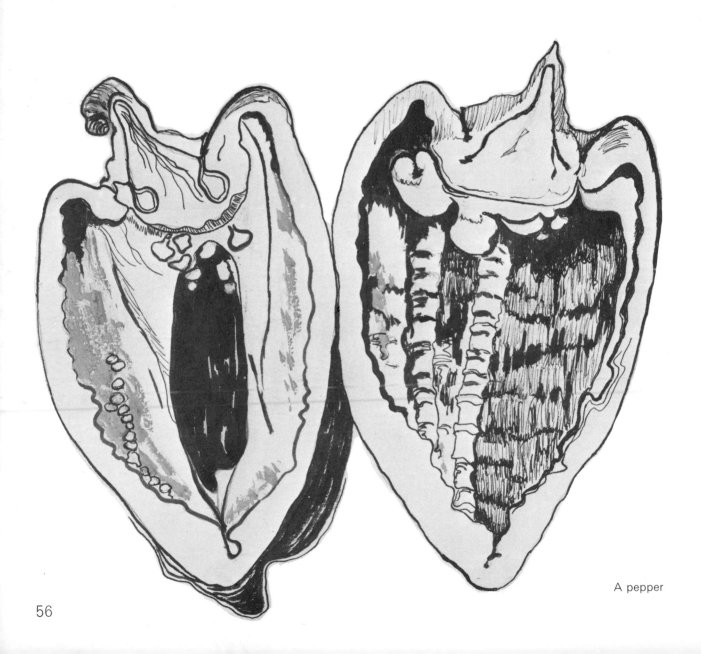

A pepper

A rose hip

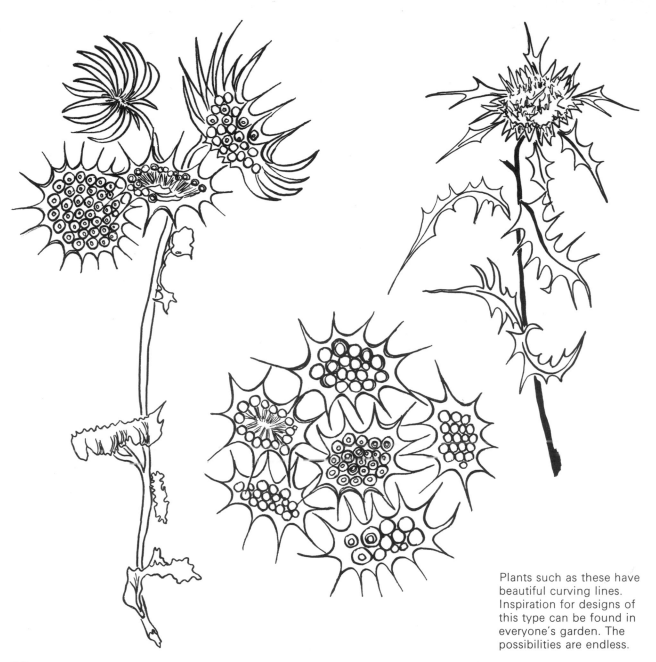

Plants such as these have
beautiful curving lines.
Inspiration for designs of
this type can be found in
everyone's garden. The
possibilities are endless.

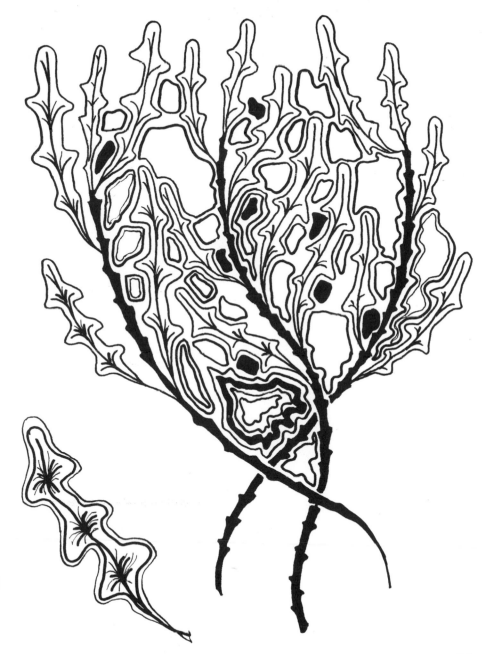

These designs have been inspired by leaf forms. The shapes have been developed around the spaces left by the leaves rather than the leaves themselves, thus giving the designs an abstract effect. This design could be worked using applied textured fabric in the dark areas and free machine embroidery for the lines.

59

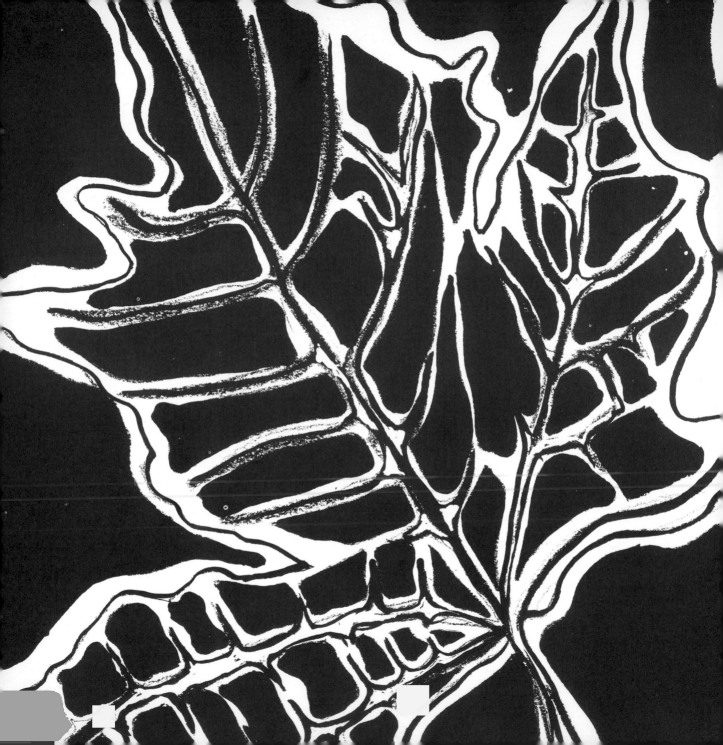

Making use of the spaces
between the leaf shapes.

61

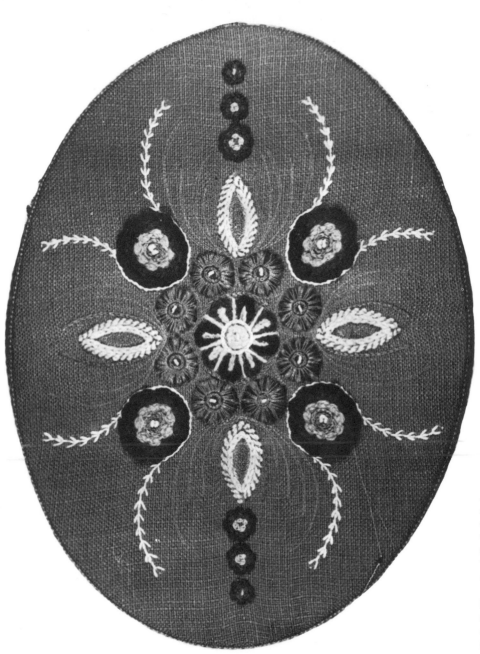

A symmetrical design is easier to create but great care must be taken to ensure that it really is symmetrical. It is essential to measure each part. This piece of work is made up of hand embroidery with very little free embroidery. It is extremely difficult to create a perfectly symmetrical piece of free embroidery.

Designs such as these can
be built up on a large scale
or worked in small detail to
decorate garments.

PLATE 3.
This is worked on a tie-and-dye fabric which can give an interesting background for a large piece of work. Here a different coloured thread was used on the bottom shuttle from the one on the top reel, and the tension loosened slightly.

64

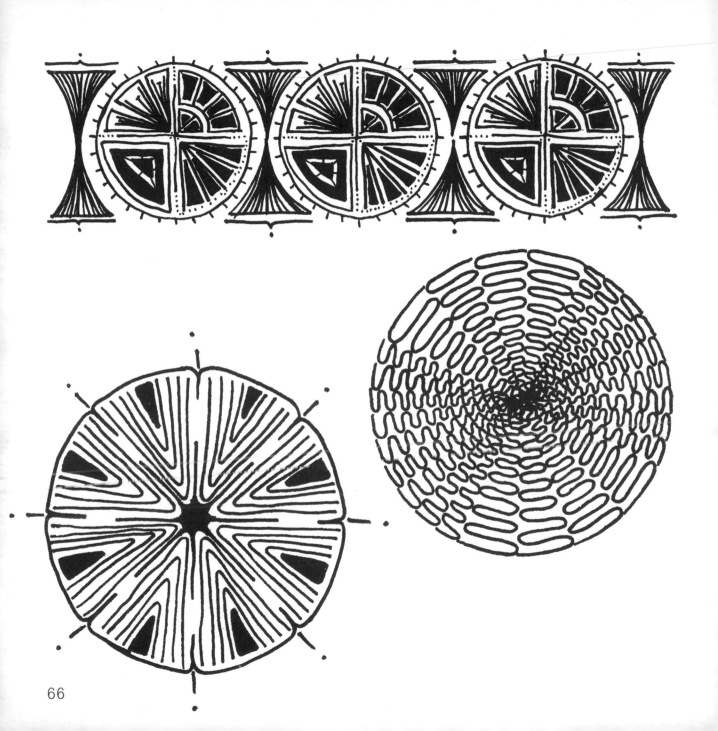

All these motifs and borders can be added directly to garments or, if preferred, machined on to separate pieces of fabric and sewn on to the garment afterwards. Border strips could be stitched on to the bottom of long skirts, for example, and motifs applied to tote bags or pockets of dresses, particularly on children's clothes.

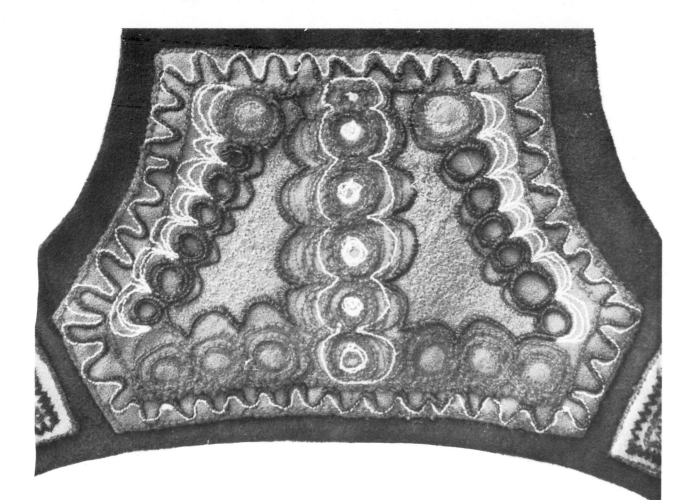

This body belt is made of dark brown suede with embroidered sections sewn on to it. All the embroidery is done on the machine, and a few beads have been added. The heavier threads are fine wool which were wound on to the lower bobbin. To do this, reverse the design in the hoop and machine from the wrong side. The heavier threads then build up on the back, which is the right side of the embroidery. Several sections are repeated; in order to do this each section must be worked simultaneously. Do not attempt to complete a section and then expect to be able to repeat it exactly. It is much better to build up each section together.

(*left*) An example of how abstract motifs can be used to decorate a body belt.

The circular shapes in this design are made with whip stitch. This is an attractive stitch made by using a loose tension on the spool or bobbin and a tight tension on the top cotton, and, if possible, a thinner thread on the spool than on the top. This stitch is only effective if a circular movement is made, because the tight top tension will then drag the loose under thread (bobbin thread) along.

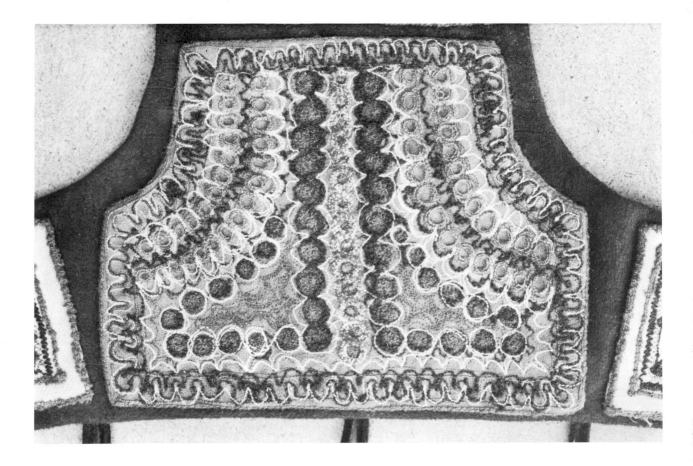

Another section of the embroidered belt.

71

Here the belt is seen worn
over a dress designed and
made by Beatrice Poulter.

(*right*) This is a complicated
design which could be made
from shapes cut out of
patterned fabrics and applied
on to a striped backcloth.
Details could be worked
afterwards on the machine.

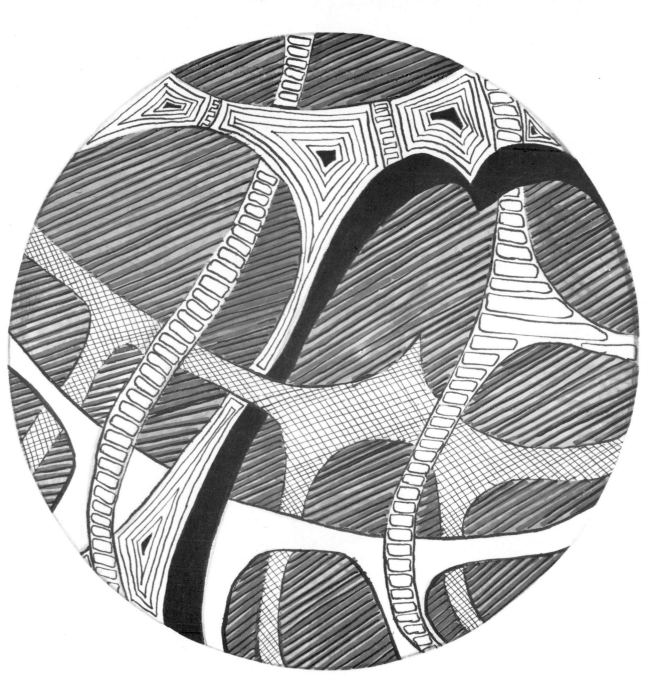

73

Designs built up from
abstract circular motifs

74

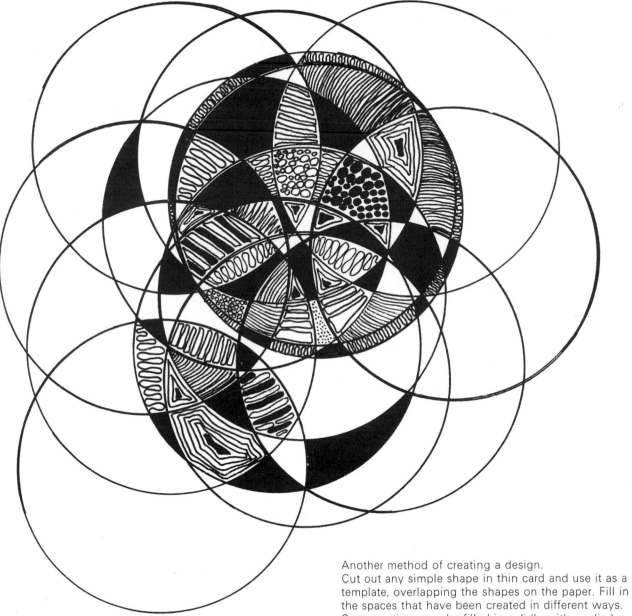

Another method of creating a design.
Cut out any simple shape in thin card and use it as a
template, overlapping the shapes on the paper. Fill in
the spaces that have been created in different ways.
Some sections can be filled in solidly with applied
fabrics. This is a simple way of developing a design
using a circle template.

Using a diamond shape as a
template.

Using a more complicated
shape.

The photographs on this
page and the following show
details of textured knitting
and crochet work. Both
these crafts can successfully
be combined with machine
embroidery in a large
piece of work. Pieces of
loosely worked knitting and
crochet can be pulled into
interesting curved shapes
and machined down on to
the background fabric,
providing additional texture
to the work.

Circular crochet motifs can also be included to good effect.

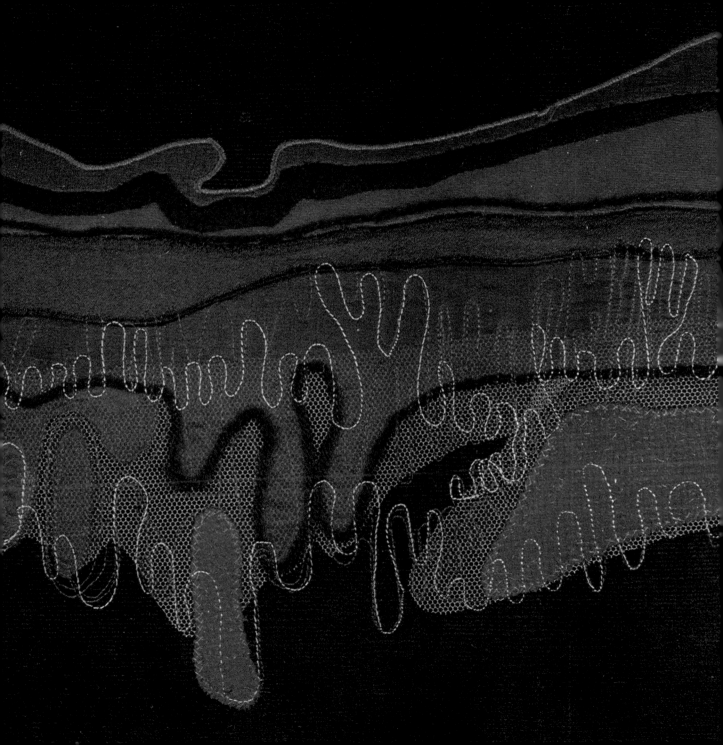

Here simple curved lines are drawn on paper and then machined on to the fabric.
Free machine embroidery fills in the spaces, also felt appliqué and hand embroidery.
Colour always plays a vital part in embroidery, and this design is worked in bright
reds and oranges with dark greens.

PLATE 4.
Reflection in water. This piece of embroidery is built up of several layers of applied
fabric, overlocking stitch and free machine embroidery.

(*right*) A simple abstract
shape worked in loose
tension machine embroidery,
hand embroidery, beads and
fringeing.

82

The following designs show ideas
that could be enlarged upon for
wallhangings or panels. They could
be worked in the sewing threads
only or combined with heavier
threads from the bobbin and hand
embroidery. Many of them may also
require appliquéed sections as well.

Both of these designs could be used as a part of a repeating pattern to make a larger design, or used alone.

If worked in certain contrasting colours, red and green for example, this design (right) could give a pulsating effect.

87

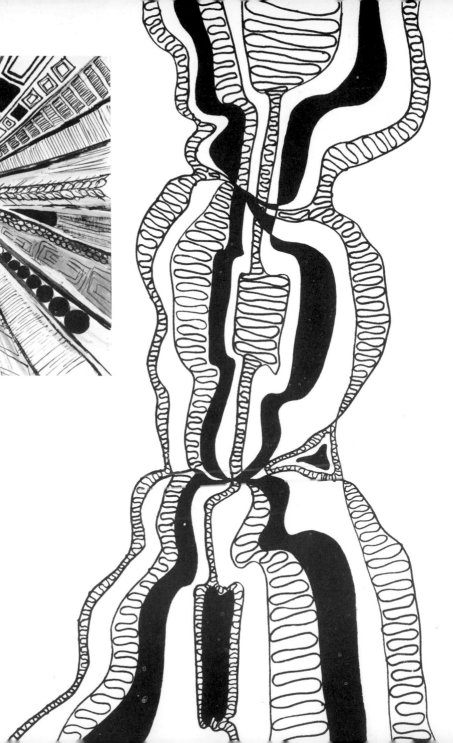

This is a good design for combining both machine and hand embroidery; the lines could be carried out on the machine while the wheat-ear shapes could be done by hand.

A design for fabric collage and machine embroidery.

88

Geometric designs such as these can be inspired by scaffolding, modern buildings, looking up into the branches of trees, and looking into intricate pieces of machinery. The illustrations on this page are good examples of this. Drawings can be done quickly with a soft pencil or piece of charcoal, as accuracy is not essential. It is probably best to draw the straight lines as one sees them, possibly missing out a few or adding some extra.

Building up a pictorial embroidery needs a great deal of careful designing beforehand because it is the tiny details that give character to the whole piece of work. Old houses, churches, castles, native dwellings and many other types of buildings are an exciting source of designs.

93

bibliography

Introducing Machine Embroidery
Ira Lillow
Batsford.

Machine Embroidery
Jennifer Gray
Batsford.

Inspiration for Embroidery
Constance Howard
Batsford.

The Young Embroiderer
Jan Beaney
Nicholas Kaye

Simple Stitches
Anne Butler
Batsford.

Design for Flower Embroidery
Elisabeth Geddes
Mills and Boon